THE BIG STORM

Books written and illustrated by Bruce Hiscock

Tundra
The Big Rock
The Big Tree
The Big Storm

ALADDIN PAPERBACKS

THE BIG STORM

written and illustrated by
BRUCE HISCOCK

First Aladdin Paperbacks edition March 2000

Text and illustrations copyright © 1993 by Bruce Hiscock

Aladdin Paperbacks
An imprint of Simon & Schuster Children's Publishing Division
1230 Avenue of the Americas
New York, NY 10020

The Library of Congress has cataloged
the hardcover edition as follows:
Hiscock, Bruce
The big storm / written and illustrated by Bruce Hiscock. — 1st ed.
p.   cm.
Summary: While describing a particuarly devastating storm that
moved across the United States, creating havoc in March-April 1982,
presents information on basic weather phenomena.
ISBN 0-689-31770-0 (hc.)
1. Severe storms—United States—Juvenile literature.
[1. Storms. 2. Weather.] I. Title.
QC943.5.U6H57   1993
551.55—dc20
92-13973
ISBN: 0-689- 83265-6 (Aladdin pbk.)

THE BIG STORM CROSSES

To my mother, Clara, and my stepdad, George, who live

beneath the big prairie sky

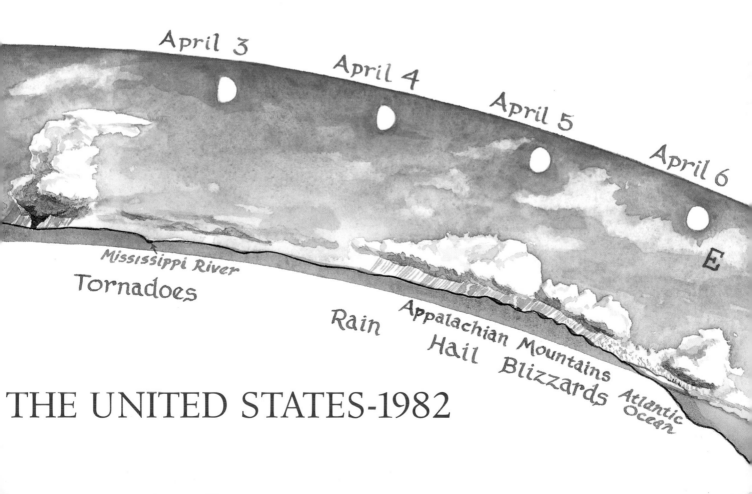

April 3

April 4

April 5

April 6

E

Mississippi River

Tornadoes

Rain

Hail

Appalachian Mountains

Blizzards

Atlantic Ocean

THE UNITED STATES-1982

It was a beautiful spring morning across most of the United States on the last day of March in 1982. The weather satellite, far out in space, showed clear skies stretching from the Rocky Mountains to the East Coast, where a few clouds lingered.

On the ground, signs of the changing season were everywhere. Flocks of geese and robins moved north as the days lengthened. Fresh new leaves covered the trees in the South, while up by the Great Lakes, spring peepers chirped from the ponds. With baseball season only a few days away, it looked like winter was finally over.

But spring is a time of rapidly changing weather. In the West a mass of clouds and cold, damp air rolled in off the ocean. It was the start of the big storm.

The clouds brought heavy rain to the Pacific Coast as the gathering storm moved inland. Like most weather systems in North America, it was carried along by the westerlies, the winds that nearly always blow from west to east across the continent.

When the storm ran up against the mountains of the Sierra Nevada range in California, the wind pushed the clouds up the steep slopes. In the cold mountain air the rain changed to snow.

W

E

SIERRA NEVADA

SPANISH
FOR

CALIFORNIA

SNOWY MOUNTAINS

It snowed hard all day in the Sierras. The flakes clung to the tall pines, coating them in heavy layers of white. But near the mountaintops, where no trees grow, the wind piled the snow into great drifts. Soon the drifts became so deep that the slopes would hold no more.

The snow began to slide from the high places, gently at first, then faster and faster, until the slides became huge avalanches. The avalanches roared down the mountains and slammed into buildings. Several people were killed.

Any storm can be dangerous as well as beautiful, but this one was a real powerhouse. And it was just getting started.

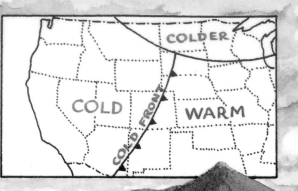

The storm moved swiftly over the Rocky Mountains, spreading blizzards from Montana to Arizona. In Colorado fierce winds gusted to 141 miles per hour, overturning vans and campers. In Nebraska the wind blew hard enough to move cow chips around.

The strongest winds came right at the leading edge of the storm. There a cold front marked the boundary between the warm springlike air covering most of the country and the cold, stormy air rushing in. Big masses of warm and cold air do not mix when they meet but instead push each other around. The line where the air masses bump is called a front.

This front was a cold front because the cold air was pushing the warm air away. Strong cold fronts usually bring high winds and sometimes violent weather.

The tremendous power of weather comes from the
sun. Our planet is surrounded by a thin layer of air called
the atmosphere, which is a mixture of gases, clouds, and
dust. Heat from the sun causes the atmosphere to flow
and swirl around the earth.

For instance, imagine that your city or county is covered
by a blanket of cool, cloudy air. No wind stirs the leaves,
and temperatures are the same everywhere.

Now let the clouds open slightly so that sunlight falls
on a plowed field or a parking lot at the mall. The sun
warms the earth or the pavement, which in turn heats
the air right above it. Hot air rises, and soon a huge
bubble of warm air is going up like an invisible balloon.

As the warm air rises, cool air flows in along the
ground to take its place, causing a breeze. Temperatures
begin to change. The sun has made the atmosphere move.

The same sort of uneven heating keeps the
atmosphere moving worldwide. Warm air rises from the
tropics while cold air flows down from the poles. This
heating pattern and others create the vast wind and
weather systems of the planet. Of course, these weather
systems change with the seasons. The long summer days
provide much more sunlight to warm and lift the air than
the short, cold days of winter.

The sun moves the weather, but the land and sea
affect it too. Ocean currents cool or warm the air. Hills
and mountains block the wind. Even the spinning of the
earth changes the wind's direction.

In fact, so many things affect the weather that when
a storm comes up, it is not easy to predict exactly what it
will do.

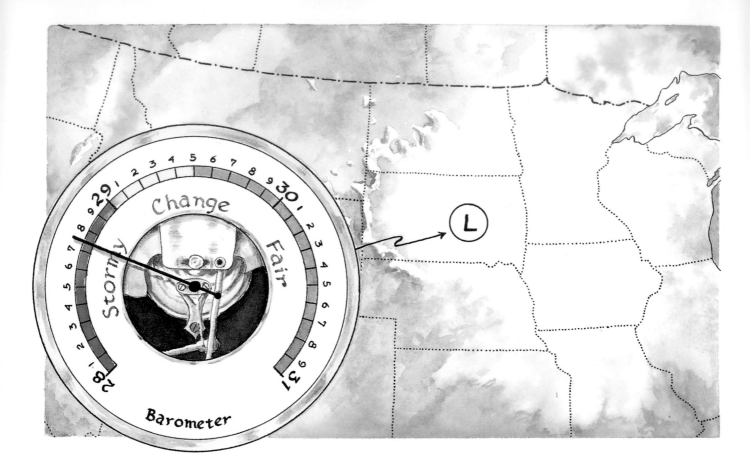

The big storm grew worse as it swept out over the Great Plains. Flocks of robins huddled on the ground, unable to fly in the blowing snow. Across the Dakotas and Minnesota, weather forecasters watched their barometers as the readings fell to record low levels. A deep low-pressure center was forming.

Barometers measure the pressure of the air directly overhead. Air, like water, has weight, and tons of air press down on the earth. This force, called barometric or atmospheric pressure, changes constantly as the air moves.

Forecasters pay close attention to these changes, for they help predict the weather to come. High pressure usually brings fair skies. Low pressure means storms, and the lower the pressure, the stronger the storm.

As the blizzard raged on, the weather stations in the storm reported the low pressure, the freezing temperatures, and the gusty wind and snow conditions to the National Meteorological Center near Washington, D.C. The data went directly into their huge computers along with data from hundreds of other weather stations, satellites, and instrument-carrying balloons.

The computer gave an overall picture of the weather to the forecasters at the National Center. Then, using more computers, they predicted what the storm would do next. These predictions were sent back to each weather station. There, a detailed forecast was made for the local area.

This work goes on every day, but with a killer storm on the loose, the forecasts were especially important.

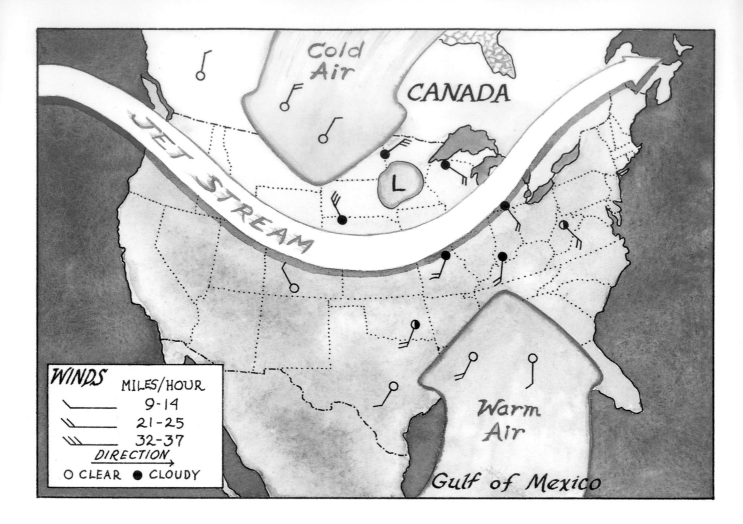

On the morning of Friday, April 2, the weather map showed strong surface winds blowing in toward the low-pressure center. Areas of low pressure push enormous amounts of air upward, causing air near the ground to rush in from all sides, like air rushing into a vacuum cleaner. Far above the surface, the jet stream, a narrow band of high-speed wind that snakes across the continent, formed a giant curve around the low.

All this was creating a huge counterclockwise swirl in the atmosphere typical of big storms. On one side of the swirl warm, moist air from the Gulf of Mexico was being drawn north. On the backside, frigid air was coming down out of Canada.

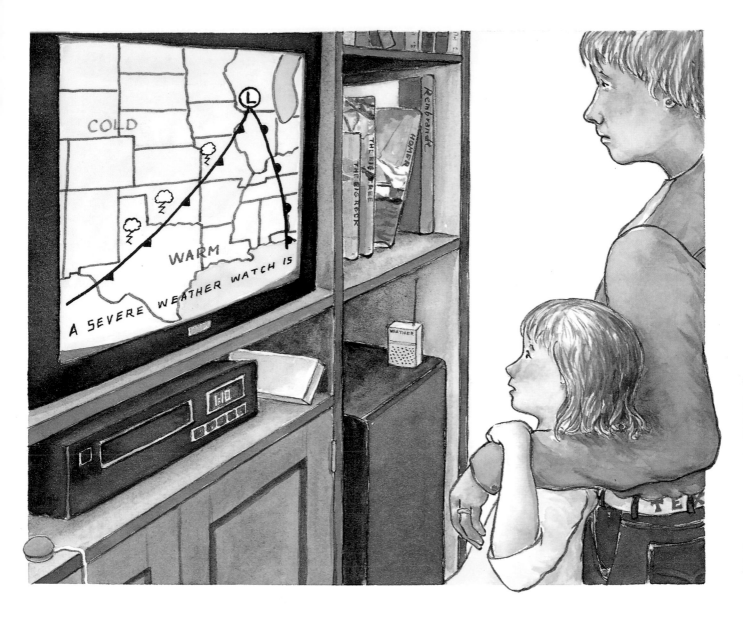

The National Severe Storm Forecast Center in Kansas City, Missouri, began plotting where these two air masses would meet. Chances were good that the collision would result in a powerful cold front, producing violent thunderstorms and tornadoes.

Local weather stations from Texas to Iowa and east were alerted. A Severe Weather Watch was announced on radio and television to warn that bad weather was possible. Forecasters checked their radar screens constantly, looking for signs of the front. Everyone waited.

The afternoon was warm and humid when a line of
towering clouds appeared across the Texas plains.
Lightning flashed in the distance. Soon the rumble of
thunder was heard. Airports closed. Dogs whined and hid
under beds. The clouds came on, churning and billowing.
An eerie darkness fell. Then slashing winds hit. Rain and
hail poured down. The cold front raced through.
Temperatures dropped sharply.

All along the front, police and other spotters watched
for tornadoes. Tornadoes are violent whirlwinds, funnel-
shaped clouds that may spiral down from thunderstorms.
They are extremely dangerous. The spotters watched
anxiously, for they knew that weather radar can pinpoint
thunderstorms but usually cannot "see" tornadoes. Eyes
are better for that.

Suddenly a tornado was sighted heading for Paris, Texas. Sirens blew. A Tornado Warning was broadcast. Families rushed for the nearest bathroom, closet, or basement shelter.

The tornado hit with the roar of a freight train. Houses and churches were torn apart. Trees shattered. Cars were tossed around.

The funnel cloud stayed down for twenty minutes, ripping a path through the city two blocks wide and five miles long. Most of the people in the path survived, though many were injured. Ten people were killed.

Tornado Areas April 2-3

More than eighty tornadoes touched down that afternoon and night in Texas, Oklahoma, Arkansas, Missouri, and other states as far east as Ohio. Even with the warning broadcasts, over thirty people died, and the damage was horrendous. The United States has more tornadoes than anyplace else in the world, but this was the worst outbreak since 1974.

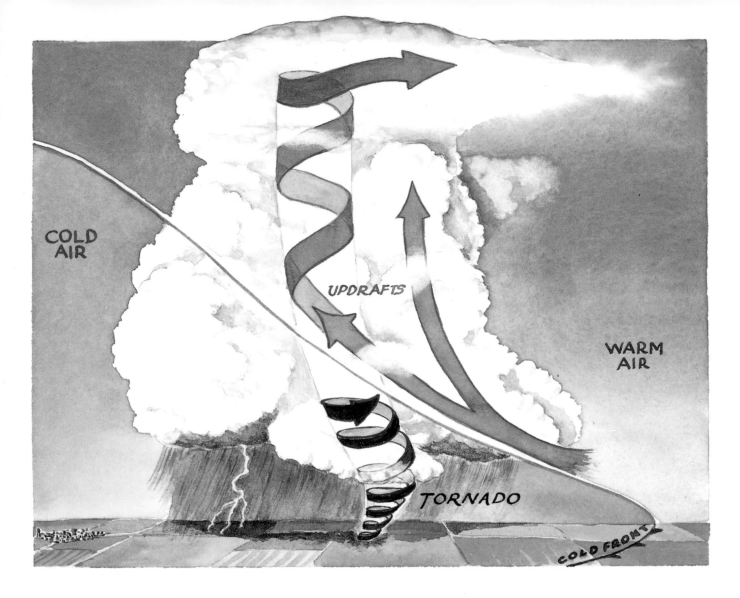

COLD
AIR

UPDRAFTS

WARM
AIR

TORNADO

COLD FRONT

Tornadoes usually form just behind a cold front as the wedge of cold, dense air pushes in, forcing the warm, moist air to rise very quickly. This produces strong updraft winds and huge thunderclouds.

If an updraft begins to spin, it may set off a tornado. Exactly what causes the spinning is not completely understood, but once the twister is formed, it sucks in air, dirt, and anything else it touches with winds of over two hundred miles an hour. Boards, bricks, and glass become deadly flying missiles. Huge funnel clouds can even lift railroad cars.

ICE CRYSTAL

SNOWFLAKE

WATER VAPOR

COLD CLOUD DROPLET

RAINDROP

When the front passed, the tornadoes stopped, but thunderstorms continued throughout the South. Heavy rain drenched Alabama and Georgia. Hail the size of golf balls dented cars and broke windows in Kentucky.

Rain and hail are formed from the moisture in clouds, but they are not simply falling bits of mist and ice. The water droplets and tiny ice crystals that make up clouds are far too small to fall by themselves, and so they remain suspended in air like fog.

Surprisingly, most raindrops start out as snowflakes. High in the cloud where the air is very cold, ice crystals gradually grow into snowflakes that are heavy enough to fall. The snowflakes then melt, if it is warm near the ground, and become raindrops. A raindrop is about a million times larger than a cloud droplet.

HAIL FORMATION

Hailstones form when an ice crystal is coated with freezing cloud mist. If a falling hailstone is lifted again and again by strong updrafts, it may become coated with many layers of ice and grow as big as a marble or even a baseball before it drops from the cloud.

All this motion of ice and water inside a cloud builds up an enormous charge of static electricity. It is just like the charge you may gather while walking across a carpet. That charge is released as a mild shock. However, when a cloud lets go of its energy, millions of volts leap out in a deadly flash of lightning. The house-shaking thunderclap that follows comes from the waves of air that expand after being heated by the electric discharge.

THUNDER

For the next three days the huge mass of Arctic air behind the cold front brought more snow and high winds to the Midwest. Driving became very dangerous. Five hundred travelers were stranded in Michigan and had to spend the night in school gyms. Rush-hour traffic in Chicago was a tangle of accidents.

The great swirl of clouds around the low was clearly
visible from space, and as the swirl drifted east, clear
skies and intense cold followed it. With no blanket of
clouds at night, the earth rapidly lost heat to outer space.
Low temperature records were set from Idaho to the
Appalachians. And still the storm was not through!

Tuesday, April 6, was opening day for the baseball season, and the New York Yankees were scheduled to play at home. The main storm center was now out at sea, but still the forecast was not good. Cold air continued to pour in, forming new lows over Pennsylvania and the New Jersey coast.

Around three in the morning, snow began to fall softly on New York City. In the Northeast the great snowstorms often begin very quietly. Soon the wind picked up. By noon it was a howling blizzard. Traffic snarled. Trains were delayed. The pace of the great city slowed to a sloppy walk.

Over a foot of snow fell in New York before the storm moved on to Boston. It was the first blizzard ever to hit New York City in April. The Yankee game was delayed for four days. Many adults said bad things about the weather, but few kids complained. They all had a day off from school.

The big storm finally ended. Snow turned to slush and melted away. People cleaned up their towns. Spring returned. Birds began traveling north again, and the evenings lost their chill.

The storm is just a memory now, but every spring the cycle repeats itself. Warm air from the south meets with cold Arctic air, triggering storms of all sizes and giving the United States one of the most varied and exciting climates on earth.